The Depression Journal

The
Depression
Journal
Creative Activities to Keep Yourself Well

CARA LISETTE and
SOPHIA KAUR BADHAN

Foreword by Dr Jonathan N. Stea
Illustrated by Victoria Barron

Jessica Kingsley Publishers
London and Philadelphia

First published in Great Britain in 2025 by Jessica Kingsley Publishers
An imprint of John Murray Press

1

A CIP catalogue record for this title is available from the
British Library and the Library of Congress

ISBN 978 1 80501 411 9
eISBN 978 1 80501 412 6

Printed and bound in Great Britain by Bell & Bain Limited

Jessica Kingsley Publishers' policy is to use papers that are natural, renewable and recyclable
products and made from wood grown in sustainable forests. The logging and manufacturing
processes are expected to conform to the environmental regulations of the country of origin.

Jessica Kingsley Publishers
Carmelite House
50 Victoria Embankment
London EC4Y 0DZ

www.jkp.com

John Murray Press
Part of Hodder & Stoughton Ltd
An Hachette Company

The authorised representative in the EEA is Hachette Ireland,
8 Castlecourt Centre, Dublin 15, D15 XTP3, Ireland (email: info@hbgi.ie)

Foreword

We live in an age where we're bombarded with information – and, unfortunately, that includes mental health misinformation. We can see it everywhere. It's in our social media feeds. It's in movies, news stories and popular culture. It even exists within our healthcare systems. It's hard to know which information we can trust when it comes to mental health. Thankfully, Cara Lisette and Sophia Kaur Badhan have gifted us a resource that we can trust.

How do I know that? Well, as a clinical psychologist, I've worked in a hospital setting for over a decade helping people who experience severe addiction and mental disorders, including depression. And I've written books about the importance of using science to help guide our treatment of mental health concerns. When I'm trying to evaluate whether a resource is trustworthy, I look to see whether it is informed by principles that have been researched and have been found to work. Those principles can be found in this book.

Specifically, the content of the book is couched in evidence-based therapeutic principles, drawing from cognitive-behavioural therapy, dialectical behaviour therapy and motivational interviewing, as well as values and meaning-based modalities. That means that you can be assured that this book has a solid foundation in science. Even better, Cara and Sophia have made these principles accessible. Sometimes evidence-based therapies can come with confusing terminology and language – Cara and Sophia have successfully extracted the helpfulness of those principles and stripped them of their psychobabble and technical jargon. In the end we're left with a book imbued with content that is accessible, easy to read and provides well-researched, practical skills to help manage depressive symptoms.

Both Cara and Sophia make it clear that this book is not meant to replace professional help, but that it can be used alongside such help. Cara calls the book 'a friend'. And I love that idea. When people feel depressed, it can be extremely difficult to do anything – even brushing one's teeth can feel like a monumental task. It can be hard to open a book, let alone write in a journal. Like Cara, I often tell my patients to think of such therapy-tasks as a friend, not a chore. Friends can help support us, ground us, act as a sounding board and help us sort through our thoughts and emotions. This book is meant to do the same – but in a more structured way.

Beyond the science, Cara and Sophia get it. They've lived and breathed depression. They understand its nature and how to successfully treat its symptoms when they become debilitating. Their empathy and compassion can be gleaned from the pages in this book, and that's ultimately why it has a friendly face.

When providing therapy to my own patients, I often recommend supplementary science-backed learning materials to help solidify the ideas we talk about during our sessions. I will be adding this book to my repertoire. I also encourage my patients to view such learning materials as a behavioural experiment. The hypothesis is that their life will improve if they participate. And so, that's my hope for you. I encourage you to conduct the experiment: use this book for five minutes every day for one month, or three months, or one year, and see what happens. See if your mood improves. And see if your life improves. If nothing changes, then you've lost five minutes every day, and I apologize. But I bet it will help. My many patients over the years have told me that when they use similar strategies and coping skills that can be found in this book it can help. And, as Sophia wisely tells us, recovery from depression is a lifelong journey with good days and bad ones – so let's keep marching forward.

Dr Jonathan N. Stea
Clinical Psychologist
Adjunct Assistant Professor, University of Calgary
Author of Mind the Science: Saving Your Mental
Health from the Wellness Industry

Hello, reader!

Welcome to your journal, which I hope will be a useful tool in managing what can be a very difficult mental health problem to live with. Throughout this book there are a number of activities to help you to explore different coping strategies, and hopefully to learn more about yourself and your experiences of depression.

Both of us are familiar with depression, and we know how difficult it can be to see a way out. We are hopeful that some of the strategies and skills in this book will help you to discover new ways to improve your wellbeing.

This book is not meant to replace medical support, but to be a friend in your journey. It's yours to use as you choose: you can write in, decorate it, draw in it. Creativity is an excellent outlet for difficult thoughts and feelings, and I hope you find some of these prompts bring you closer to your goals.

The exercises we have included are based on our own experiences, using both Cara's knowledge as a mental health professional and both of our experiences of depression.

We hope that you are able to get what you want out of this process, and that it helps you in your ongoing journey of living the life you want to live.

Never forget that you are more than your depression, and that you deserve to live a full and happy life.

Lots of love, Cara and Sophia

A note from Sophia

Hello! I'm Sophia and I have been living with depression since the age of 11. My turning point came around six years ago, when I was 15 and reached crisis. I had absolutely no hope for my future. I couldn't see a way out, and I'd just completely given up. I remember thinking 'Is this really it? Isn't there more to life than feeling so awful all the time?' And it was awful. So I decided I was tired of feeling that way. I was sick of being sick, and I was going to fight for my life back. Rediscovering who I was amongst all of this was tough. I didn't know who I was without it. It took many months – well, years, actually, and lots of hard work. There were so many times when I was ready to give up, but I picked myself back up, again and again. I see my recovery as an ongoing, even lifelong journey. I have ups and downs, good days and bad days, but I am determined to keep travelling forwards, not backwards.

I now use my lived experiences to advocate for youth representation, engagement and involvement in sectors such as healthcare, politics and education. I am an award-winning youth activist and campaigner, and I've worked with organizations such as Public Health England, the NHS and UNICEF UK.

Never in a million years did I imagine I would be living the life I am now. I didn't even think I deserved to get better, let alone that it was even possible.

I saved my own life. I hope this journal helps you to save yours.

All my love, Sophia x

Focus on the step in
front of you, not the
whole staircase

My goals for the future

Start by setting yourself some goals. What would you like to achieve by using this journal, and by when?

1. ....
   ....

2. ....
   ....

3. ....
   ....

4. ....
   ....

5. ....
   ....

6. ....
   ....

7. ....
   ....

8. ....
   ....

9. ....
   ....

10. ....
    ....

My reasons to keep going

What motivates you to keep going when things feel difficult? You can refer back to this list any time you need a reminder.

1. ....
....

2. ....
....

3. ....
....

4. ....
....

5. ....
....

6. ....
....

7. ....
....

8. ....
....

9. ....
....

10. ....
....

What is depression?

Depression is a common mental health problem characterized by low mood, which in turn leads to symptoms like a lack of motivation, disrupted sleep, appetite changes and poor self-esteem.

Everybody feels sad sometimes, but it might start to become a problem if it's prolonged and interfering with daily life, such as work, self-care and relationships.

As well as low mood, people with depression can often experience other emotions such as guilt, hopelessness and loneliness. Some people describe feeling numb and having an absence of recognizable emotions. People might find that they are losing interest in things they used to enjoy, feeling very tired and lethargic, having difficulties concentrating and sometimes thoughts about self-harm or suicide.

It's important to remember that depression is a treatable illness and, although it can feel hopeless, it is absolutely possible to be well and live a happy and fulfilling life.

How does your body feel when you're depressed?

As we've just discussed, although a depression is a mental health problem, it can often be felt in the body. How does your body feel when you're depressed? Try drawing those feelings out.

Daily mantras

I deserve to live a life without the weight of depression

I deserve to get better, however that may look for me

Recovery is not linear, and healing takes time

This may be the hardest thing I will ever do, and
it will also be the best thing I will ever do

Sometimes we just have to sit in the sunlight
and wait for our leaves to unfurl

I will fight for myself and the life I deserve to live

Everything I need is within me. I know what I
need, and I will take care of myself

I deserve the love I keep trying to give everyone
else – I won't give up on myself!

This is tough, and I am tougher

There is more to life than this. Keep on keeping
on. The world is waiting for ME!

Hot cross buns

Our thoughts, feelings and behaviours all connect to one another. The way we behave can affect how we think and feel, and trying to change our thinking can impact what we do and what emotions we are experiencing.

For example, if we hear a noise in the night and our first thought is that someone has broken in, we are likely to feel scared and possibly hide away. If our thought is that a pet knocked something over, we are more likely to feel annoyed, and probably go back to sleep. There's lots of different ways our thinking and behaviour can impact our mood.

When you're feeling depressed, what thoughts go through your mind? How do you behave? How does this impact how you feel? Try mapping it out on the hot cross bun below.

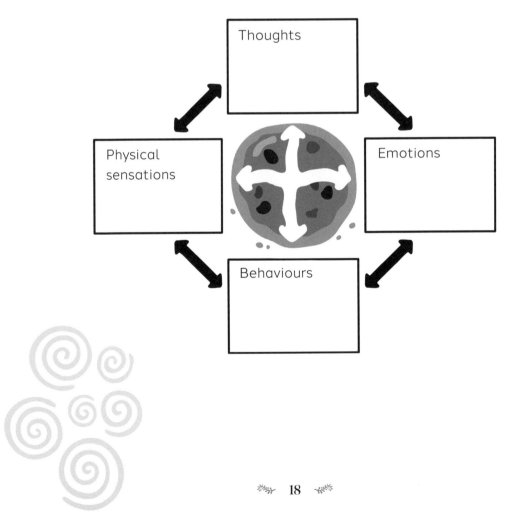

Now have a think about an alternative. How could changing your behaviour or challenging some of the thoughts that arise when your mood is low influence how you feel?

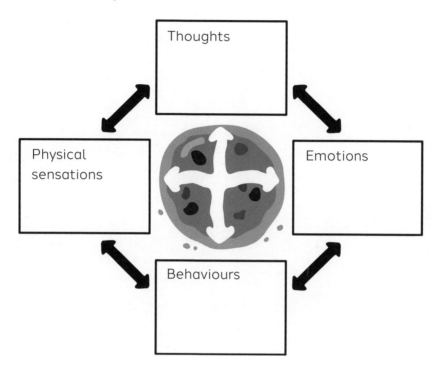

Why do I want to stay well?

What are your reasons for wanting to focus on keeping yourself well?

....

....

....

....

....

....

....

....

....

....

....

....

....

....

....

....

....

....

....

What does depression look like to you?

It can be really helpful when trying to challenge depression to think of it as something separate from us. What does your depression look like, and what does it say to you?

You are worth the
time it takes to do the
things that heal you

Useful distractions

Distractions can be a really useful tool in managing short-term difficult thoughts and feelings. There are some suggestions here that might help, but you will probably have some of your own too.

- ❀ Word games
- ❀ Having a bath
- ❀ Jigsaw puzzles
- ❀ Watching your favourite series
- ❀ Learning an instrument
- ❀ Painting
- ❀ Practising new hair styles
- ❀ Reading poetry or short stories
- ❀ Writing calligraphy
- ❀ Taking care of plants
- ❀ Doodling

Distractions that help me

You might already have your own ideas for distraction techniques that help you. Write down some ideas that you could try if you need to take your mind off things.

1. ....
   ....

2. ....
   ....

3. ....
   ....

4. ....
   ....

5. ....
   ....

6. ....
   ....

7. ....
   ....

8. ....
   ....

9. ....
   ....

10. ....
    ....

How are you feeling today? Draw or write it out!

My support network

It's important to reach out for help when we are struggling, whether that be to friends, family, mental health professionals or charities, for example. Have a think about who is in your network and who you can reach out to when you need support.

Friends:

....

....

....

Family:

....

....

....

Professionals:

....

....

....

Other:

....

....

....

Brain dump

How are you feeling right now? Sometimes getting our thoughts out onto the page can help us to process and make sense of them.

....

....

....

....

....

....

....

....

....

....

....

....

....

....

....

....

....

....

....

Pros and cons of change

Sometimes trying to challenge mental health problems and be well requires a lot of hard work and can feel impossible. Lots of us who are going through this process feel this way at times. This exercise is helpful to remind you why you have started this journey to improving your wellbeing.

What are the pros of changing?

....

....

....

....

....

....

....

What are the cons of changing?

....

....

....

....

....

....

....

What are the pros of not changing?

. . . .

. . . .

. . . .

. . . .

. . . .

. . . .

. . . .

What are the cons of not changing?

. . . .

. . . .

. . . .

. . . .

. . . .

. . . .

. . . .

What is important to me?

When we are struggling with our mental health it can be really difficult to remember what is important to us. Try and make a list of things that are important to you.

1. ....
....

2. ....
....

3. ....
....

4. ....
....

5. ....
....

6. ....
....

7. ....
....

8. ....
....

9. ....
....

10. ....
....

What are my values?

Our values guide the way we behave, both towards others and towards ourselves, and they can help us set goals and recognize where we would like to make changes to our lives. It can be useful to identify our values as this can help us to establish changes we want to make, so we can align our actions closer to the things that are important to us. Here is a list of values that you might connect with. It might help to highlight some, but there is also space to record your own that don't feature here.

Acceptance	Friendship	Maturity
Achievement	Fun	Morality
Adventure	Generosity	Nourishment
Balance	Growth	Nurture
Beauty	Health	Optimism
Bravery	Happiness	Order
Caring	Honesty	Popularity
Community	Hope	Productivity
Compassion	Independence	Quality
Connection	Individuality	Quiet
Creativity	Inner peace	Recreation
Dedication	Intelligence	Reflection
Determination	Joy	Responsibility
Discovery	Justice	Security
Empowerment	Kindness	Spirituality
Equality	Knowledge	Stability
Faith	Learning	Success
Family	Love	Teamwork
Freedom	Loyalty	Tolerance

Trustworthiness	Vitality	Wisdom
Truthfulness	Wealth	Youthfulness
Unity	. . . .	. . . .
. . . .	. . . .	. . . .
. . . .	. . . .	. . . .
. . . .	. . . .	. . . .
. . . .	. . . .	. . . .
. . . .	. . . .	. . . .
. . . .	. . . .	. . . .
. . . .	. . . .	. . . .
. . . .	. . . .	. . . .
. . . .	. . . .	. . . .
. . . .	. . . .	. . . .

How closely am I living by my values?

Try to pick the top ten values that are most important to you and think about how closely you are living by them at the moment.

What is the value?	How important is it? (1–10)	How closely am I living by it? (1–10)

What changes can I make that will bring me closer to living a life aligned with my values?

....
....
....
....
....
....
....
....
....
....
....
....
....
....
....
....
....
....
....

This is just one chapter, not the whole story

The depression cycle

When our mood is low, we can often feel unmotivated, lethargic and withdrawn. This can lead to a reduction in our level of activity, for example we might isolate ourselves socially, stop engaging in hobbies we once enjoyed and even stop attending to important tasks like eating and drinking enough, going to work or education or paying our bills. However, this then results in us getting stuck in a cycle. What we know is that the more we withdraw from activities, the worse our mood gets. It's completely natural to think that we will start doing these things again once our mood is better, but what we actually need to do is to start engaging in different activities first, in order to improve our mood.

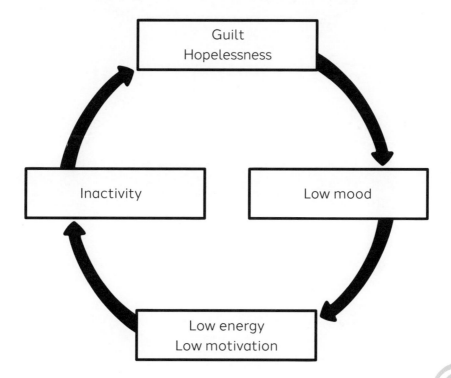

Rather than wait for our mood to improve, we actually need to start doing these actions first. This can feel totally unnatural and go against everything that our minds and bodies feel like they want to do, but it's a really effective way of improving our mood and helping us to regain some energy.

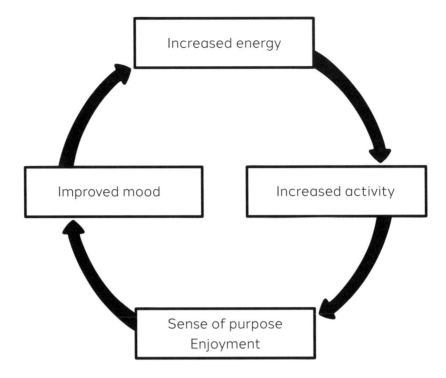

We can break activities down into different categories, for example those which we enjoy, including hobbies and socializing, versus those that are more essential life activities such as taking medication or eating regularly. You can sort your activities into whichever categories work for you, but these lists might be a helpful guide. Once we have worked out what falls under each category, we can start planning them into our day. It is best to include a mix of different activities, both leisure and essential. There will also be some that you find easier to do when you are feeling tired and flat, and others that require a bit more energy to do.

Activities I enjoy

1. ....
   ....

2. ....
   ....

3. ....
   ....

4. ....
   ....

5. ....
   ....

6. ....
   ....

7. ....
   ....

8. ....
   ....

9. ....
   ....

10. ....
    ....

Activities I need to do

1. ....
....

2. ....
....

3. ....
....

4. ....
....

5. ....
....

6. ....
....

7. ....
....

8. ....
....

9. ....
....

10. ....
....

Low energy activities

1. ....
   ....

2. ....
   ....

3. ....
   ....

4. ....
   ....

5. ....
   ....

6. ....
   ....

7. ....
   ....

8. ....
   ....

9. ....
   ....

10. ....
    ....

High energy activities

1. ....
   ....

2. ....
   ....

3. ....
   ....

4. ....
   ....

5. ....
   ....

6. ....
   ....

7. ....
   ....

8. ....
   ....

9. ....
   ....

10. ....
    ....

Using ACE to plan my week

What's really important when planning your week is to have a combination of ACE activities. To balance your week try to include activities that give you a sense of Achievement, Closeness and Enjoyment. There might be some that give you a high sense of enjoyment, such as watching your favourite film, but a low sense of achievement. That's okay, because we can balance that with tidying the lounge, which might create more of a sense of achievement but isn't as fun. It also really helps to have activities that give you a sense of closeness with other people, such as meeting up for coffee or having a nice phone call. A mix of activities that incorporate all these elements is key to helping improve low mood.

Scheduling my week

There are lots of different ways to schedule your time. Some people find it easier to do it a day at a time, others a week at a time, and you might prefer to do it hour by hour or break it down in to bigger chunks. Here is a guide to get you started.

	Monday	Tuesday	Wednesday
Morning activities			
Afternoon activities			
Evening activities			

Thursday	Friday	Saturday	Sunday

Rewards

Doing things that feel really difficult deserves recognition. What are some ways you can reward yourself when you've tried to fight against your depression and make positive changes? Remember sometimes it's the effort that counts, rather than the outcome. Being kind to yourself can often feel unnatural when struggling with low mood, but it's important to start recognizing that you do deserve nice things.

....

....

....

....

....

....

....

....

....

....

....

....

....

....

....

....

Brain dump

How are you feeling right now? Sometimes getting our thoughts out onto the page can help us to process and make sense of them.

....

....

....

....

....

....

....

....

....

....

....

....

....

....

....

....

....

....

....

....

Signs I am feeling depressed

How do you know when you are feeling low in mood? What do you, and those around you, need to look out for?

....

....

....

....

....

....

....

....

....

....

....

....

....

....

....

....

....

....

What can I do to help myself when I am feeling depressed?

How can other people help me when I am feeling depressed?

Collage making

As you might have found for yourself as you've starting working your way through this book, creativity can be a really helpful way to express how we feel and give us something to focus on. Making a collage of emotions using different magazines and newspapers can be a cathartic way to get our feelings out and share how we are feeling with others if we choose to share it.

You didn't come this far,
to only come this far

How are you feeling today? Draw or write it out!

Coping statements

When we are depressed, it can feel like those feelings are going to last forever. Here are some things you can say to yourself to get you through.

1. Anything is better than nothing.

2. This is tough, and you are tougher.

3. Hold on until tomorrow.

4. Let yourself rest.

5. You got this.

6. Allow yourself a little moment of joy – there are glimmers of hope everywhere.

7. You have survived all of your darkest days. You have done this before, and you can do it again.

8. Give yourself love.

9. You may have depression, but depression sure as hell does not have you.

10. Minute by minute, hour by hour, day by day.

Letter writing

When we feel low, it's really common to start feeling negatively towards ourselves and about life in general. What would you like to say to yourself when you next feel this way? What would be important to remember?

....

....

....

....

....

....

....

....

....

....

....

....

....

....

....

....

....

....

....

....

The power of music

Music can be an amazing tool for our wellbeing, and there are so many inspiring songs and artists out there. The type of music we listen to can have a big impact on our mood, and it would be helpful to think about what songs might help you when you need a bit of motivation, as well as those that inspire you to keep going.

My motivational playlist

....

....

....

....

....

....

....

....

Songs that inspire me

....

....

....

....

....

....

....

Quote jar

Inspirational and motivational quotes can be a really nice way to start the day, or give you a little pick-me-up when you're feeling low. It can also be helpful to get suggestions from other people of reminders they'd like you to have on bad days. Find a nice glass jar or box and try making a list here of the messages you could include. Then you can take one out whenever you need a boost.

....

....

....

....

....

....

....

....

....

....

....

....

....

....

....

....

....

Brain dump

How are you feeling right now? Sometimes getting our thoughts out onto the page can help us to process and make sense of them.

....

....

....

....

....

....

....

....

....

....

....

....

....

....

....

....

....

....

....

....

Things I like about myself

Low self-esteem is often something that occurs alongside mental health difficulties. Try to think of some qualities you like about yourself that you can reflect on in future.

1. ....
....

2. ....
....

3. ....
....

4. ....
....

5. ....
....

6. ....
....

7. ....
....

8. ....
....

9. ....
....

10. ....
....

Things other people like about me

It can also be helpful to reflect on things other people value in us, as they may be different to our own ideas. Ask the people around you what they like about you – some of the answers might surprise you.

1. ....
   ....

2. ....
   ....

3. ....
   ....

4. ....
   ....

5. ....
   ....

6. ....
   ....

7. ....
   ....

8. ....
   ....

9. ....
   ....

10. ....
    ....

31 days of self-care

1 Make yourself your favourite non-alcoholic drink and focus on it completely	2 Write a love letter to yourself	3 Give yourself a massage – use your fingers to ease the tension in your neck and move around your scalp in small, circular motions
8 Have a solo dance party!	9 Give yourself a hug	10 Wash your bedding and towels with your favourite detergent
15 Bake something nice	16 Have a dinner date with yourself – light some candles and remind yourself that you're worthy of nourishing food	17 Lay out a blanket and stargaze or watch the clouds
22 Let yourself cry	23 Visualize showing up as the highest version of yourself, however that may look	24 Write a letter to your younger self
29 Treat yourself to fresh flowers	30 Change your underwear – you deserve care, cleanliness and comfort	31 Forgive yourself

4 Stretch your body in whatever way feels good	5 Give yourself permission to rest	6 Call a friend or loved one, or a helpline to chat to	7 Listen to a song and sing all the words, even if you get them wrong!
11 Have an 'everything' shower	12 Make a blanket fort and embrace your inner child!	13 Make a conscious decision to pick up a book instead of your phone	14 Plan a movie night, either by yourself or with friends
18 Stop whatever you are doing and drink a full glass of water	19 Create a fruit platter for yourself – in some cultures preparing fruit for loved ones is a sign of affection and caring	20 Take yourself on a walk, take a drink with you and put on a podcast or listen to nature	21 Turn off your phone for 24 hours
25 Write a positive affirmation and stick it on the bathroom mirror	26 Write down who and what are important to you and why	27 If you're struggling to get out of bed, just put your feet on the floor – you're one step closer	28 Set a timer and do as many little tasks as you can in that time

Self-care activities

It can feel difficult to look after ourselves when we are struggling with our mental health. One of the best ways to challenge this is to start being kind to ourselves. What self-care activities can you try?

1. ....
   ....

2. ....
   ....

3. ....
   ....

4. ....
   ....

5. ....
   ....

6. ....
   ....

7. ....
   ....

8. ....
   ....

9. ....
   ....

10. ....
    ....

Miracle question

If you were to wake up tomorrow and your depression was gone, what would life look like? What would you be doing, how might you be thinking differently?

....
....
....
....
....
....
....
....
....
....
....
....
....
....
....
....
....
....

How are you feeling today? Draw or write it out!

Hope scrapbook

Low mood can often result in feelings of hopelessness, and it can be really difficult to pay attention to the positives. Try getting a scrapbook and filling it with things that give you hope. It might be goals for the future, kind things other people have said about you, things that remind you of people you care about. You could fill it with memories of when you've been happy before or reminders of how you've come through difficult times in the past. Look back at it when you're starting to feel hopeless and demotivated, as a reminder of all the reasons to keep going.

Give yourself the
future you deserve

Why do I want to stay well?

What are your reasons for wanting to focus on keeping yourself well?

....
....
....
....
....
....
....
....
....
....
....
....
....
....
....
....
....
....
....

Current coping strategies

It's likely that over time you will have picked up some coping strategies for when things get difficult. However, it's important to remember that these might not always be healthy or beneficial to us in the long term, even though they might help us in the short term. Hopefully, you will also have some that are helpful for you in both the immediate and the future. Have a think through the coping strategies you currently use, and whether these are helpful for both present and future you.

Coping strategy:

....
....
....

Short-term pros:

....
....
....

Short-term cons:

....
....
....

Long-term pros:

....
....
....

Long-term cons:

....
....
....

Coping strategy:

....
....
....

Short-term pros:

....
....
....

Short-term cons:

....
....
....

Long-term pros:

....
....
....

Long-term cons:

....
....
....

Coping strategy:

....
....
....

Short-term pros:

....
....
....

Short-term cons:

....
....
....

Long-term pros:

....
....
....

Long-term cons:

....
....
....

Coping strategy:

....
....
....

Short-term pros:

....
....
....

Short-term cons:

....
....
....

Long-term pros:

. . . .

. . . .

. . . .

Long-term cons:

. . . .

. . . .

. . . .

New coping strategies

Are there any coping strategies that you haven't tried yet, that you think might be helpful? List them below and revisit this page next time you feel you need it.

1. ....
....

2. ....
....

3. ....
....

4. ....
....

5. ....
....

6. ....
....

7. ....
....

8. ....
....

9. ....
....

10. ....
....

54321 grounding technique

Depression can feel completely overwhelming sometimes. If you find yourself feeling like this, this technique can be very effective at bringing you back into the here and now by helping you to connect to your senses. There are five steps to follow.

1. Look around you and notice **five things you can see**. This could be a painting, a plant or a person, for example. Pay attention to what each of these things look like: their shapes, colours and sizes.

2. Focus on **four things you can feel**. This could be the wind, your clothes against your skin, the floor underneath your feet. Notice the different textures and sensations.

3. Name **three things you can hear**. Maybe there are birds chirping outside, or cars passing in the street. Perhaps you can hear a TV show in the background. Focus on the different tones and volumes.

4. Notice **two things you can smell**. Have you used a nice fabric softener on your clothes, or are you wearing your favourite perfume? Maybe you are outdoors and can smell plants and flowers.

5. Think about **one thing you can taste**. Perhaps you have chewing gum or a cup of tea nearby. If you can't taste anything, try to imagine what one of your favourite things tastes like.

My skills and strengths

Everybody has their own individual strengths that we can draw upon when things feel difficult. What are some of yours? If you feel stuck, it can help to ask the people around you their thoughts.

1. ....
   ....

2. ....
   ....

3. ....
   ....

4. ....
   ....

5. ....
   ....

6. ....
   ....

7. ....
   ....

8. ....
   ....

9. ....
   ....

10. ....
    ....

Brain dump

How are you feeling right now? Sometimes getting our thoughts out onto the page can help us to process and make sense of them.

....

....

....

....

....

....

....

....

....

....

....

....

....

....

....

....

....

....

....

....

Sleep hygiene

Sleep hygiene is just a term that means 'good sleeping habits'. I'm sure you know how important regular sleep is, but it can be a difficult thing to do in practice when we have busy lives. Depression can have a really big impact on sleep cycles – often people end up sleeping too much or not enough, and the pattern can become really disrupted. This can have a knock on effect on mood.

The most helpful thing to do is get yourself into a consistent bedtime routine. This should occur at the same time every night, if possible. Prior to going to bed you should try to avoid large meals, caffeine and blue light from electronics such as phones or tablets.

It can also help to do calming activities such as having a bath, reading and turning down very bright lights.

Getting exercise during the day can also help with falling asleep, in addition to a dark, quiet room which is at a comfortable temperature.

It's important to try to wake up at the same time every morning too, and to avoid taking naps during the day, as this helps get us into a regular sleep cycle.

Are there any changes you think you need to make to your bedtime routine? Think about how you could improve your sleep.

What could your helpful bedtime routine look like?

....

....

....

....

....

....

....

....

There's a past version
of you who is so proud
of your progress

Motivational poster

Being able to visualize the reasons why we are getting out of bed every day and trying to make positive changes can be really powerful. Try reflecting back on the reasons you've given yourself earlier on in this journal, and see if you can find anything that visually represents them – photos, magazine cut-outs, drawings. Then arrange them into a poster you can display in your house. It might be beneficial to think about where in the house you are likely to struggle the most. For example, if getting out of bed is your biggest hurdle, your bedroom wall might be a good place. If you find nourishing yourself really hard, try sticking it to a kitchen cupboard. Wherever works best for you.

Square breathing technique

Square breathing has been shown to be helpful when trying to relax and feel calm, and is an exercise that can be used wherever you are. Find a window, a wall, a painting, or any other square shape you can see to focus on. If you can't see one, you can use your index finger to trace one in front of you.

Slowly trace your eyes across the top of the square in front of you, breathing in for a count of four. As you scan down the right side of the square, hold your breath for a count of four. Breathe out for a count of four as you trace the bottom of the square, then hold for a count of four as you scan up the left-hand side. Repeat this as many times as necessary, breathing in a slow and controlled way.

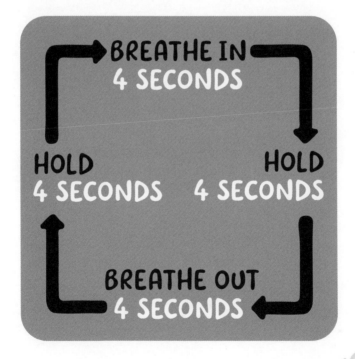

BREATHE IN
4 SECONDS

HOLD
4 SECONDS

HOLD
4 SECONDS

BREATHE OUT
4 SECONDS

Quotes, lyrics and phrases that inspire me

....

....

....

....

....

....

....

....

....

....

....

....

....

....

....

....

....

....

....

....

....

Thinking traps

Most of us have unhelpful thinking habits that we have developed over our lives that can sometimes get in the way when we are feeling distressing and difficult emotions. These are some of the most common ones that people experience.

Mind reading:

Assuming we know what other people are thinking.

Example: 'They all think I am stupid.'

Ask yourself: Am I making assumptions about what they are thinking?

Prediction:

Thinking we know what's going to happen in the future.

Example: 'I am going to fail that assignment.'

Ask yourself: How likely is it that this is going to happen?

Comparing and despairing:

Only seeing the positives in others then comparing ourselves against them negatively.

Example: 'I am rubbish at drawing compared to them.'

Ask yourself: Am I focusing on others rather than myself?

Mental filter:

Only noticing what we want to notice and filtering out everything else that doesn't fit that narrative, like sieving out all the positives and only letting the negatives through.

Example: Only noticing things we consider to be our failures and ignoring any successes.

Ask yourself: Am I only noticing the bad things?

Mountains and molehills:

Exaggerating the negatives and minimizing the positives.

Example: Thinking the negatives are worse than they are and the positives are less significant than they are.

Ask yourself: What would somebody else say about this situation?

Critical self:

Putting ourselves down and blaming ourselves for things that are not our fault; also referred to as the 'internal bully'.

Example: 'The group project not going well at work is all my fault.'

Ask yourself: What role did others play in this situation?

Shoulds and musts:

Putting pressure on ourselves and having unreasonable or unrealistic expectations of what we should or shouldn't be doing.

Example: 'I should be good at this by now.'

Ask yourself: Is this an unrealistic expectation I am setting for myself?

Black and white thinking:

Thinking that things can only be right or wrong, good or bad, with nothing in between.

Example: 'If I don't do this perfectly then I have failed.'

Ask yourself: Is it possibly to do everything perfectly all of the time?

Catastrophizing:

Believing or imagining only the worst possible case scenario.

Example: 'This is going to be a disaster.'

Ask yourself: What are some other possible outcomes to this situation?

Labelling:

Giving labels to others or to ourselves.

Example: 'I am an idiot.'

Ask yourself: What would somebody else say in this situation?

Emotional reasoning:

Assuming our feelings are always rational, for example 'I am anxious so I must be in danger.'

Example: 'I feel ashamed so I must be a bad person.'

Ask yourself: Does feeling bad mean something is bad?

Overgeneralizing:

Noticing a pattern based on one situation or drawing wide-ranging conclusions.

Example: 'Nothing good ever happens.'

Ask yourself: What positive things have happened?

Personalization:

Taking responsibility or feeling a sense of blame for something that may not be your fault.

Example: 'It's my fault that my friendship group fell out.'

Ask yourself: Were there any other factors involved in this situation happening?

Everybody has their own individual traps – you might find some of these don't apply to you at all and others make complete sense. It might be helpful to think about which of them feel relevant to you, and situations where you think they might arise. For example, if you find yourself feeling very anxious about things that could happen in the future, you might be 'catastrophizing' or 'predicting'. The more you start to recognize your own thinking traps, the more you can start to challenge them.

What are my unhelpful thinking styles?

....

....

....

....

....

....

....

....

....

....

....

....

....

....

....

....

....

....

....

....

When might I notice them?

How does this affect me?

....
....
....
....
....
....
....
....
....
....
....
....
....
....
....
....
....
....
....
....

Negative automatic thoughts

There are three types of automatic thoughts: positive, neutral and negative. Most people will experience a mix of all of these, however when people are depressed negative automatic thoughts can become overwhelming. This is the terminology we use to describe the negative self-talk that goes on in our brains when we don't feel good, and these thoughts often perpetuate the low mood. If you're constantly having thoughts that you're stupid, unlikeable or unworthy, it's only natural that it's going to have a knock on effect on how you feel. Equally, when people are feeling low they are much more likely to experience these thoughts. This is another unhelpful cycle that can be formed when people are depressed. The way to challenge this is first to start noticing the thoughts, and then catch them as they arise.

The next step is to recognize what thinking trap you might be falling into, as we covered on the previous pages. Then you can start to actively challenge the thought.

Taking your thoughts to court

To find out whether our NATs are true, we need to start gathering evidence. There are lots of different questions we can ask ourselves in this process, such as:

What is the evidence that my thought is true?

Is there any evidence my thought might not be true?

How would I know if this thought was true?

Are there any facts I've overlooked?

How realistic is it that this thought is true?

Is there any other explanation?

How might somebody else view this situation?

Are there any other ways I can view the situation?

How might I think differently about this if I wasn't depressed?

Is thinking this way helpful or unhelpful to me?

Now it's time to take your thought to court, using the template on the following page.

Judge: What is the thought?

. . . .

. . . .

. . . .

How strongly do you believe the thought? (0–100%)

. . . .

Defence: Why is this thought true? What factual evidence is there?

. . . .

. . . .

. . . .

Prosecution: Why might this thought not be true?

. . . .

. . . .

. . . .

Jury: What is the final conclusion? Who is telling the truth?

. . . .

. . . .

. . . .

How strongly do you believe this thought to be true now? (0–100%)

. . . .

What could an alternative thought be?

. . . .

. . . .

. . . .

How are you feeling today? Draw or write it out!

How to make a self-soothe box

Self-soothe boxes, also referred to as crisis boxes or sensory boxes, are excellent tools to have access to. They are designed to be full of items that help you to get through periods of distress. Try and fill yours with things that cater to each of your five senses. Here are some suggestions of things you could include that might be helpful:

- ❊ **Taste:** Chocolates or mints, or maybe your favourite tea bags

- ❊ **Smell:** Essential oils, nice hand creams or perfume

- ❊ **Touch:** Stress balls, tangles or something soft like a small cuddly toy

- ❊ **Hear:** A prompt card to remind you to access your happy playlist or favourite song

- ❊ **See:** Photos of people you love, motivational quotes or perhaps some letters of encouragement

It might also be helpful to keep a list of distractions, helplines or apps that you find useful when you are finding things difficult.

What will go in my self-soothe box?

. . . .

. . . .

. . . .

. . . .

. . . .

. . . .

. . . .

. . . .

. . . .

. . . .

. . . .

. . . .

. . . .

. . . .

. . . .

. . . .

. . . .

. . . .

. . . .

. . . .

Communicating with others

When we are struggling with our mental health, we can often end up isolating ourselves from others. This can make it difficult for people to help us, because they either don't know we are feeling this distress, or they aren't sure exactly how to help.

When you are finding things difficult, how could you communicate with people about how you are feeling?

....
....
....
....
....
....
....
....
....
....
....
....
....
....
....
....
....
....
....

Nature as therapy

Although nature alone is not a cure for depression, being outside can be a calming way of centering ourselves and connecting with the world around us. Try going for a short walk or spending time in the garden if you have one. If you don't, consider travelling somewhere nearby that allows you to breathe some outside air.

If this feels too difficult or you don't have easy access to outdoor space, try getting something for your house that helps you connect to nature, such as a small plant, or sitting by the window.

Coping with suicidal thoughts

Although not true of everyone who lives with depression, some people will experience suicidal thoughts. These can be passive, in the form of not wanting to be here any more, or more active such as making plans to end their life.

Feeling suicidal can be an incredibly dark place to be, however it's likely these thoughts are temporary.

One of the most helpful things to do when experiencing suicidal thoughts is to share them with somebody. This could be family, a friend, a health professional or a helpline. There is always somebody out there to listen on the end of the phone, even when you may be feeling totally alone.

If thinking about the future feels too overwhelming, try to focus on just getting through the next hour, and then maybe the next day. Set small, achievable goals and actions for yourself that feel manageable and keep you safe.

Try getting yourself to somewhere where you feel safe, and stay away from things you could use to harm yourself. Try to use some of the distractions and grounding techniques in this book, and remember that this feeling will pass. Although your situation is individual and unique, you are not alone in how you feel.

TIPP skills

Sometimes when we are really distressed, we need quick and easy interventions to help us break the cycle and tolerate our emotions. This is where TIPP skills (temperature, intense exercise, paced breathing, paired muscle relaxation) can be useful. TIPP skills are part of dialectical behaviour therapy, and they can help you when you are feeling lots of different emotions at once or when you are at a crisis point.

Temperature

Changing the temperature can help us gain clarity and decrease the intensity of our emotions. By introducing your body to something cold, you initiate what is called the 'dive response'. This is a physiological response where your blood pressure drops and your heart rate slows down, forcing your body to calm down. Cold can be a shock to your body at first, so it may take 15–30 seconds for the dive response to kick in. Sophia's favourite technique is to run her hands and wrists under cold water. You can also put cold water in a ziplock bag and hold it to your face or squeeze ice.

Intense exercise

When you are feeling revved up, angry or frustrated, engage in intense exercise for a short period of time. Try doing 15 star jumps or running on the spot. This can help expend pent-up energy in a more positive way and provides an outlet for negative emotions.

Paced breathing

Sometimes when our body thinks we are in danger, we need to show it that we are safe. One way to do this is paced breathing – where you breathe out for longer than you breathe in. It may take some practice to find what works for you. Try starting with breathing in for three seconds, holding for one second and then breathing out for four seconds. Sophia finds it helpful to rationalize with her brain, repeating to herself that if she is safe enough to take the time to breathe like this, then she is safe. You could also try paced breathing in combination with paired muscle relaxation.

Paired muscle relaxation

This skill is great for when you are in public or even dealing with difficult emotions before bed. The idea is that you tense your muscles while you breathe in, and relax them as you breathe out. Sophia finds this works best for her hands and feet – it is easy to clench your fists or curl your toes and they then feel much better when relaxed.

Noticing the positives

When feeling depressed, it can give us tunnel vision to the good things around us. Noticing positives in the day can be a useful tool to help us reframe some of that negative thinking. For the next week, try and notice at least one positive thing that has happened over the course of the day.

Day one:

....

....

....

....

Day two:

....

....

....

....

Day three:

....

....

....

....

Day four:

....
....
....
....

Day five:

....
....
....
....

Day six:

....
....
....
....

Day seven:

....
....
....
....

How did you find it trying to notice the positives? Did it get easier? Did you feel any better by the end of the week?

What would I say to a friend if they were going through this?

Experiencing depression, which can affect many areas of our lives and those around us, can often result in feelings of guilt, and we can be harder on ourselves than we need to be. It's also easy to be unkind to ourselves when we are feeling low. Remember, it's not your fault that you have a mental health problem. What would you say to a friend if they were going through something similar?

....

....

....

....

....

....

....

....

....

....

....

....

....

....

....

....

....

Brain dump

How are you feeling right now? Sometimes getting our thoughts out on to the page can help us to process and make sense of them.

....

....

....

....

....

....

....

....

....

....

....

....

....

....

....

....

....

....

People who inspire me

We can draw inspiration from lots of different places, but sometimes having people we look up to can be really helpful. Who inspires you to be your best self?

1. ....
   ....

2. ....
   ....

3. ....
   ....

4. ....
   ....

5. ....
   ....

6. ....
   ....

7. ....
   ....

8. ....
   ....

9. ....
   ....

10. ....
    ....

Problem solving

Low self-esteem and poor motivation can make us doubt our ability to problem solve. This can result in avoiding things and not putting ourselves out there, because we fear we can't cope and feel overwhelmed. There are some helpful strategies to learn how to problem solve effectively, and in turn this helps us feel more confident in our abilities to be able to do difficult things. Try thinking of a problem and using the template below to create a mind map of all the different possible solutions. They can be as realistic or as silly as you like, but try to think of as many as you can and add your own spider legs to the diagram.

Problem solving mind map

Problem solving table

Now choose the top three possible solutions from the mind map, and break them down. Think of the pros and cons of each, and then choose the outcome based on the one that makes the most sense to you. This is an exercise you can practise any time you feel overwhelmed.

What is the problem?		
What is a potential solution?	**What are the benefits to this?**	**What are the cons of this?**
What solution have I chosen and why?		

Checking in with myself

It's not uncommon to find it difficult to pin down or connect with how we are feeling, which can make it difficult to spot early warning signs of relapses. The following steps can help you to notice how you might feel at that moment.

- ❃ What am I feeling in my body right now?

- ❃ What emotions can I feel right now?

- ❃ What thoughts are going through my mind at this moment?

- ❃ What am I doing now?

- ❃ What do I want for myself going forward?

Positive words wordsearch

The first three words you see are your words of the day.

P	S	H	I	Y	O	J	H	P	Z	H	Y	D	S
T	L	U	M	R	A	U	Q	H	O	S	G	L	E
A	H	K	K	O	Q	P	A	P	S	N	R	Y	L
H	H	G	V	J	O	I	E	E	J	C	E	L	F
R	M	R	I	Z	E	N	N	Y	G	S	N	W	C
W	E	N	G	L	X	L	O	R	J	N	E	J	O
X	A	S	X	W	U	L	A	G	C	I	K	Q	M
F	R	J	I	F	A	T	W	P	U	E	N	Z	P
L	P	T	D	L	I	D	X	E	Q	C	Z	D	A
Q	S	N	I	T	I	W	Z	A	K	G	B	I	S
D	I	I	U	E	P	E	X	C	L	D	R	J	S
M	Y	D	D	S	N	U	N	E	U	B	H	G	I
W	E	U	R	E	T	J	E	C	H	U	X	J	O
N	O	I	T	A	N	I	M	R	E	T	E	D	N

RESILIENCE
PEACE
HOPE
DETERMINATION

LIGHT
ENERGY
MINDFULNESS
SELF-COMPASSION

GRATITUDE
JOY

Depression meals

Something you may struggle with when feeling low is making food for yourself. It can feel too overwhelming to prepare something, cook it and then clean up, so you may turn to processed food or even neglect eating altogether. Fighting depression can take a lot of energy, so it is important you fuel your body and your mind to give you the best chance at recovery. There are also things that you can do to make life easier in difficult moments, such as pre-preparing food, or investing in a micro-wave or airfryer. These things mean there is less cleaning up to do, which is always a plus! Here are some relatively easy, fairly nutritious meals for when you need to eat but can't manage a huge task.

- ❀ You can make scrambled eggs in the microwave! Crack some eggs into a bowl, add whatever seasonings you have and microwave for 30 seconds at a time, stirring in between. You'll have soft, fluffy scrambled eggs in three minutes with no pan to wash! Pair this with some toast for a full meal.

- ❀ Always keep some bread in the freezer. You can defrost it in the toaster or microwave, and it lasts much longer than fresh bread.

- ❀ Try microwaving a jacket potato. Make sure you stab it with a knife first so that it doesn't explode, and then microwave it for 5–6 minutes, turning halfway through. A good tip is to keep tinned protein in the cupboard, such as tuna or beans, so that you can chuck those on top and have a decent meal with little effort.

- ❀ For when you can't remember the last time you ate vegetables – keep some microwaveable vegetable packets in the freezer. Snip a hole in the top and microwave them for a couple of minutes. You can spruce them up with salt and pepper, butter, cheese or even just eat them as they are!

- ❀ Crackers and cereal bars are always good to have on hand for when you are particularly low energy. You can also eat crackers with a dip. If you can't get individual packs of crackers, try to put the rest in a ziplock bag or an airtight container once you're done so they don't go soft.

* For times when you have a bit more energy, batch cook some pasta sauce and then freeze it in individual portions. You can add whatever you like – veg, protein, seasonings – and when you're struggling all you have to do is boil some pasta to serve it with!

* The above also goes for soups – easy to take out and eat with some bread from the freezer.

Remember – you deserve to fuel your body and your mind. Eating something is better than eating nothing at all!

Letter writing

Living with depression can frequently bring up lots of emotions for us, and there are often lots of negative thoughts swimming around. If you could write a letter to your depression, what would you say?

....

....

....

....

....

....

....

....

....

....

....

....

....

....

....

....

....

....

Managing triggers

We all have triggers that can lead to lapses and relapses, and it's important to remember that different situations and experiences are likely to contribute to low mood. Writing them down can help us to recognize them, so we can then learn to challenge and cope with them when they arise. We can't avoid triggers forever, but what we can try to do is learn to cope with them.

What are my triggers?

....

....

....

....

....

....

....

....

....

....

....

....

....

....

....

....

....

How can I cope with my triggers?

Once we have identified triggers, we can start to notice them more. The world can be a difficult place at times, and sometimes we are going to come across things that trigger us. How can you cope with or manage yours?

....

....

....

....

....

....

....

....

....

....

....

....

....

....

....

....

....

There are better
things ahead than what
we leave behind

Early warning signs

Sometimes – often, even – it can feel like a low episode has come out of nowhere. However, it's likely that there are some early warning signs that a lapse or relapse is approaching, even if we don't always realize it. What do you think you, or those around you, might notice ahead of this happening?

Early warning signs that I am becoming depressed

....

....

....

....

....

....

....

....

....

....

....

....

....

....

....

My traffic lights

Sometimes it can be helpful to think of our progress in terms of a traffic light system: red meaning relapse, orange meaning we need to be careful and pay more attention to our thoughts and feelings, and green meaning we are well and happy. Have a think about what life looks like for you in each of these zones and what your plan of action would be for each one.

What does my green zone look like?

....
....
....
....
....
....
....

How can I stay in this zone?

....
....
....
....
....
....
....

What does my orange zone look like?

....
....
....
....
....
....
....

How can I get out of this zone?

....
....
....
....
....
....
....

What does my red zone look like?

....
....
....
....
....
....
....

How can I get out of this zone?

....

....

....

....

....

....

....

How are you feeling today? Draw or write it out!

Keeping myself safe

꙳꙳꙳꙳꙳꙳꙳꙳꙳꙳꙳꙳꙳꙳꙳꙳꙳

Although this doesn't apply to everybody, when we are struggling there are times when there may be risks to our safety. If this applies to you, what do you think those risks are and how can you keep yourself safe?

....

....

....

....

....

....

....

....

....

....

....

....

....

....

....

....

....

....

....

Crisis planning

It's perfectly possible that our mood will fluctuate without resulting in a crisis, however it's important to be prepared should that situation arise. Have a think, either alone or with people around you, about how you would manage if you felt you were in crisis, and what that means to you.

What signs should I be aware of if I am heading to a crisis?

....

....

....

....

....

....

What signs should other people be aware of if I am heading to a crisis?

....

....

....

....

....

....

What can I do to manage this without needing direct support from another person?

....
....
....
....
....
....

Who can I contact if I am in crisis?

....
....
....
....
....
....

What do I need from those people?

....
....
....
....
....
....

Where can I go if I am in crisis?

....

....

....

....

....

....

How can I keep my environment safe if I am in crisis?

....

....

....

....

....

....

Brain dump

How are you feeling right now? Sometimes getting our thoughts out on to the page can help us to process and make sense of them.

....

....

....

....

....

....

....

....

....

....

....

....

....

....

....

....

....

....

....

Good things don't come
from comfort zones

Managing setbacks

Depression can come and go across our lifetime, and it's likely we are all going to have things that happen in our lives that require us to use our coping skills, whatever those may be. Have a think about what might lead to a setback for you, and how you would manage it.

What could cause a setback?

....

....

....

....

....

....

....

....

How could I manage this?

....

....

....

....

....

....

....

....

Keeping well

There are lots of things we need to do to keep ourselves on track, some every day and some less often. Have a think about what some of these are for you.

What can I do on a daily basis to keep myself well?

....
....
....
....
....

What can I do on a weekly basis to keep myself well?

....
....
....
....
....

What do I need to do less often to keep myself well?

....
....
....
....
....

What have I achieved since starting this journal?

I hope that, over the time you have been working through this book, you have been able to start thinking more about ways you can cope with depression, and how to help yourself when you feel low. What are some of the things you have achieved, no matter how big or small, since you started using this journal?

....

....

....

....

....

....

....

....

....

....

....

....

....

....

....

....

....

Congratulations, reader!

You've worked your way through this journal. We hope that you have found some of these exercises useful and that they have got you thinking about ways you can live the life you deserve.

There are ways you can continue seeking support, which we will add to the back of this book.

We wish you all the luck in the world for your life beyond this journal. Remember, you are worthy of a full and happy life. Be kind to yourself.

Lots of love, Cara and Sophia

Useful Resources

Websites and helplines

Mind: www.mind.org.uk / 0300 123 3393

Samaritans: www.samaritans.org / 116 123

Books

Reasons to Stay Alive by Matt Haig

Broken by Jenny Lawson

The Stranger on the Bridge by Johnny Benjamin

The Things You Can Only See When You Slow Down: How to Be Calm in a Busy World by Haemin Sunim

The CBT Art Workbook for Depression by Jennifer Guest

Acknowledgements

Cara

Thank you to everybody who believes in my books and has supported this journal series from the start. It has evolved into something magical, and I hope this journal can reach the people who need it. As ever, thank you to my support network, who are always there through the ups and downs and cheer on my creative projects.

Lastly, thank you so much to Sophia for all the contributions she has made to this book – it is all the richer and more special because of you.

Sophia

Thank you to Cara and Jessica Kingsley Publishers for this opportunity – I can't believe my name is on the cover of a book!

Thank you to everyone who has believed in me from day one – Amanda, Mr Heppel, Tracy, Bob and everyone at the #iwill Movement – I wouldn't be here without you all and I'm forever grateful for the friends I have made along this journey.

Shoutout to Adela for letting me use her brainpower!

And, most importantly, a special thank you to Mumma and Dadda for always standing by me and cheering me on, wherever life has taken me.

About the Authors

Cara Lisette has struggled with her mood from her early teens, predominately with depression until a diagnosis of bipolar disorder until her mid-twenties. She is familiar with how it feels to be depressed, and with support she has learned how to manage low episodes, and how to be kind to herself during lapses.

Cara has long been creative and kept journals for many years, and has found solace and value in creativity as a way to express thoughts and feelings. It is through doing this that she discovered how this could impact her ability to recognize when she's struggling, and the different strategies that she uses to keep well and live the life she wants to live.

She put this book together in the hope that others would discover the role that creativity can play in maintaining positive mental health, and that it might help people to learn more about themselves and their depression, and in turn learn skills to cope when things do get difficult.

Cara is also a registered mental health nurse and qualified psychological therapist, so throughout this book you will find exercises and tools that she has not only found helpful in her own journey but knowledge she can draw upon from her experiences working as a mental health professional. She is the author of *The Eating Disorder Recovery Journal*, *The Bipolar Journal*, *The OCD Recovery Journal* and *The Anxiety Recovery Journal*.

She runs a successful blog (www.caras-corner.com) about her experiences with mental illness and can be found on Twitter and Instagram at @caralisette, where you can follow her progress in more detail and keep up to date with her other projects.

Sophia Kaur Badhan BCAh FRSA is an award-winning mental health activist with lived experience. She has worked with organizations nationally and internationally to promote youth voice. Sophia is a recipient of the 1317th Points of Light Award, and the Diana Award, which is the highest international accolade a young person can receive for their humanitarian aid and social action. She also received the British Citizen Award for her services to healthcare and has been recognized by the British prime minister.

Sophia believes in the #PowerOfYouth and is a vocal advocate for person-centred, trauma-informed mental healthcare practices. She manages her depression by finding ways in which she can make everyday tasks easier, and therefore less daunting. Her motto is 'anything is better than nothing', and she takes each day as it comes, doing little things to make life more manageable for her future self. Alongside Cara, Sophia hopes this journal will help equip people with the skills to manage their depression and live a life worth living.

Discover more books from this series...

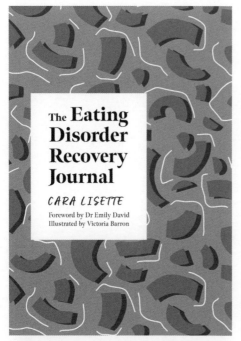

The **Eating Disorder Recovery Journal**

CARA LISETTE

Foreword by Dr Emily David
Illustrated by Victoria Barron

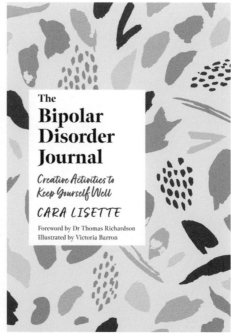

The **Bipolar Disorder Journal**

Creative Activities to Keep Yourself Well

CARA LISETTE

Foreword by Dr Thomas Richardson
Illustrated by Victoria Barron

The **OCD Recovery Journal**

Creative Activities to Keep Yourself Well

CARA LISETTE and PHOEBE WEBB

Foreword by Ashley Fulwood
Illustrated by Victoria Barron

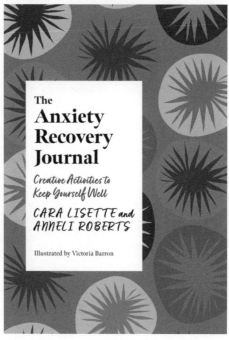

The **Anxiety Recovery Journal**

Creative Activities to Keep Yourself Well

CARA LISETTE and ANNELI ROBERTS

Illustrated by Victoria Barron